REBECCA LENKIEWICZ

Her Naked Skin

faber and faber

First published in 2008
by Faber and Faber Limited
3 Queen Square, London WC1N 3AU

Typeset by Country Setting, Kingsdown, Kent CT14 8ES
Printed in England by CPI Bookmarque, Croydon, Surrey

A CIP record for this book
is available from the British Library

ISBN 978-0-571-24146-0

2 4 6 8 10 9 7 5 3 1

For my mother, Celia (Mouse)

Acknowledgements

I would like to thank Howard Davies, Nick Hytner,
Mel Kenyon, Dinah Wood, Sebastian Born
and Chris Campbell for their support and insight
in the writing and production of this play.

And many thanks to Nina Steiger, Matthew Hollis,
John Light, Emma McNally, Celia Mills,
Periwinkle and David Unwin and Beverly Cook
of the Museum of London variously for
writing spaces, archives, music, material, inspiration.
And to Peter Quint thanks as ever.

Her Naked Skin was first performed in the Olivier auditorium of the National Theatre, London, on 24 July 2008. The cast was as follows:

Celia Cain Lesley Manville
William Cain Adrian Rawlins
Eve Douglas Jemima Rooper
Florence Boorman Susan Engel
Mrs Schliefke Pamela Merrick
Emily Wilding Davison Zoë Aldrich

House of Commons

Herbert Asquith David Beames
Miss Brint Harriette Quarrie
John Seely Julien Ball
Augustine Birrell Ken Bones
Edward Grey Simon Markey
Keir Hardie Robert Willox

Holloway Prison

Potter Tony Turner
Mrs Briggs Stephanie Jacob
Dr Vale Dermot Kerrigan
Dr Parker Nick Malinowski
Nurse Elicia Daly
Young Nurse Stephanie Thomas
Wardress Ruth Keeling
Guard Edward Newborn
Guard Joe Dunlop

Charlie Power Gerard Monaco
Hunt Julien Ball
Brown Tony Turner
Doctor Klein Ken Bones
Mrs Collins Deborah Winckles
Lord Curzon David Beames
Robert Cecil Robert Willox
Mrs Major Barbara Kirby
Felicity Anna Lowe

Other parts played by members of the Company

Director Howard Davies
Designer Rob Howell
Lighting Designer Neil Austin
Projection Designer Jon Driscoll
Music Harvey Brough
Sound Designer Paul Groothuis
Assistant Director Elly Green

Characters

Celia Cain
forties

Florence Boorman
seventies

Eve Douglas
twenties

Mrs Schliefke
sixties

Mrs Briggs
twenties

Miss Brint
twenties

Mrs Collins
sixties

Emily Wilding Davison
forties

Mary Nicholson
twenties

Clara Franks
twenties

William Cain
forties

Charlie Power
twenties

Brown
forties

Hunt
forties

Keir Hardie
fifties

Herbert Asquith
sixties

John Seely
fifties

Edward Grey
fifties

Augustine Birrell
fifties

George Curzon
fifties

Robert Cecil
fifties

Dr Klein
forties

Dr Vale
thirties

Dr Parker
twenties

Potter
thirties

**Guards, Nurse, Suffragettes,
Wardresses and MPs**
Parts may be doubled/tripled

The action takes place in London in 1913

HER NAKED SKIN

'I freeze and yet am burned'
Elizabeth I

Act One

SCENE ONE

A parlour. Morning. Emily Wilding Davison sits, dressed to go outside. She stands and puts a sash around her waist in front of a mirror. She turns on the gramophone. A contemporary song plays. She checks herself in the mirror and touches the lining of her jacket. The gramophone gets stuck. She does not move. She checks the lining of her jacket again. She takes the needle off the record, checks her purse, goes to the mirror, puts on her hat and checks the inside of her jacket. She picks up a rolled piece of paper then leaves with it in her hand.

The sound of a gramophone needle on a cracked old record going round, loud.

On a large screen we see the Derby of 1913. The horses race around Tattenham Corner and a small grainy figure comes onto the track and is trampled underfoot. The image is almost impossible to make out but the general impression of the film is that something has 'happened'.

SCENE TWO

The House of Commons. A private room. Afternoon. Some of Asquith's cabinet sit at a large table, smoking, drinking. It is an informal summoning of Liberal MPs. Birrell and Grey pass round photographs and newspapers. Seely enters and takes a seat.

Seely Temperature's gone sky high, no?

Birrell Thought we had a cold, turns out to be a fever.

Seely At least they've laid on a drink.

3

Grey Has anyone actually talked to him yet?

Seely I just passed him on the stairway. He looked like it was war to the knife.

Grey Curzon's gone loco about it too. Says we should deport them.

Seely Yes. Well. Curzon.

Asquith enters. He is with a young female secretary, Miss Brint.

Grey Sir.

Asquith Grey.

Asquith sits. Miss Brint sits apart from the MPs.

So? What are we thinking?

Seely It'll burn itself out, H.H. A few days of women keening, then it'll die down.

Asquith I think you're being optimistic.

Birrell I'm with you. I don't think it's going away. It's all dependent, of course.

Asquith Yes. Quite.

Birrell Hardie will jump on it tomorrow.

Grey If it becomes heated in the House, Seely simply comes in with the Irish.

Seely There's enough to come in with.

Grey examines the picture.

Grey Pluck.

Asquith What?

Grey Got to give it to her. The girl has pluck.

Asquith I don't believe her pluck is in dispute. Any word, Miss Brint?

Brint Miss Davison's unlikely to survive the day, sir.

Asquith That's . . . unfortunate.

Grey Damn miracle the gal's lasted this long.

Asquith Bugger. There'll be a major funeral, no?

Birrell It'll be women as far as the eye can see.

Asquith Which should sound like heaven, but it doesn't.

Quiet smiles and chuckles at the PM's wit.

Grey Our man at Poplar says they're planning a march, thousands of them.

Asquith A touch tasteless. And premature. What does the *Post* say?

Birrell examines its front page.

Birrell Queen enquired about Miss Davison's progress last night. They're calling the latest attacks an 'epidemic'.

Grey They scorched my golf course, did I tell you? Acid all over the grass. Rare finches there, too. I don't expect they relished the amazon invasion.

Birrell (*reads*) 'Militant suffragism is like a pain in the body . . . monomania.'

Asquith You say she's tried it before?

Asquith looks to Miss Brint who looks to her notes.

Brint Yes, sir. From the prison balcony. Twice.

Grey Hysterical.

Asquith That's what we'll have to concentrate on. Her lack of . . .

Birrell A horse? Sorry, just came out.

Seely If we brand her a hysteric we may suffer a backlash.

Birrell The real problem is, the public will renew their focus on the forcible feeding.

Asquith Hospital treatment, Birrell.

Birrell Call it what you like. There'll be a new stink all over again. If this woman dies they've got their first bona fide martyr. It may well blow their non-violent manifesto to kingdom come.

Seely I think you're being a touch dramatic.

Birrell They keep comparing their campaign to the Irish. Look where that's headed.

Asquith The Irish are the Irish. And they've been damned useful to us. What we're dealing with here is a lunatic fringe of lonely frigid women who crave attention. Anything new from the police?

Brint They found a return ticket in her purse, sir. And a diary entry for next week.

Pause. Hard thought while Asquith refills his glass.

Seely That's rather good, isn't it? Ergo, she didn't mean to die for the cause at all. She stepped out onto the track by mistake.

Brint What?

Seely What?

Brint Nothing. Sorry, sir.

Grey My mother had no sense of direction whatsoever. Still stretching it a bit though, isn't it?

A few stolen looks behind Brint's back. Veiled chuckles.

Seely People run out onto the course after all the horses have gone by.

Birrell You're saying she might not have seen forty thoroughbreds racing round Tattenham Corner at full pelt?

Seely I'm saying she was endeavouring to celebrate in the traditional fashion. But was a little premature. What do you think?

Asquith pours himself a stronger drink.

Asquith Maybe she'll live. That would be better, wouldn't it? (*Pause.*) Wouldn't it?

Seely Absolutely. Of course. It would be wonderful. Preservation of human life aside, which we all pray will happen, it would . . .

Grey Indicate a botch job. Universal female incompetence. Present company excepted. Right up to the tenth hole they scorched it. Rotten.

Asquith You're right, Seely. People will see it as nothing compared to Ireland. So who's making the big noise about Home Rule tomorrow?

SCENE THREE

Regent Street. Evening. Celia Cain stands near a shop front. There are various women, looking in windows, along the street. A Flower Lady stands next to a Newspaper Vendor. Eve Douglas watches Celia.

Celia Do you have the time upon you, please?

The Vendor gets out his watch.

Vendor Just coming up to six.

Celia How many minutes to six?

Vendor How many? . . . Seven.

Celia Thank you. I'll have a paper, please.

Celia gives the Vendor a coin and takes the paper. Eve approaches Celia.

Eve Excuse me. Are you? . . . Sorry. Nothing.

Celia Yes. I expect I am.

Eve Oh.

Celia Yes.

Celia walks away from Eve and approaches the Flower Seller.

I'll have some violets, please.

Flower Seller Ta.

The Flower Seller wraps some violets for Celia, who takes them and walks away. Eve approaches Celia again.

Eve I'm . . . I . . .

Celia What? Is it your first time? I promise it won't hurt.

Eve I don't think I can do it.

Celia Excuse me.

Celia walks away from Eve and stands near another shop. Celia looks at the newspaper, distracted. She puts the newspaper under her arm, waits. Eve watches her, then takes out a hammer and smashes the window in front of her.

Eve I did it. I did it.

Celia Yes. You're a touch bloody early, but you did it.

Celia takes out a hammer from her coat and smashes the shop window in front of her. The other women in the street follow suit. Windows are being smashed simultaneously throughout the West End.

SCENE FOUR

Florence, Mrs Schliefke and other Suffragettes line up in front of a prison guard, Potter, who sits at a table and writes down their details. Once they have answered Potter's questions they go to a set of scales and are weighed. A Guard records their weight. Then on to another table where a Guard issues them with items such as a toothbrush and a handkerchief.

Potter Name?

Mary Nicholson Mary Nicholson.

Potter Occupation.

Mary Nicholson Factory worker.

Potter Sentence.

Mary Nicholson Seven months. Windows.

Potter Name.

Clara Franks Clara Franks.

Potter Occupation.

Clara Franks Student of fine art.

Potter Sentence.

Clara Franks Six months.

Potter Name.

Florence Florence Dorothy Mary Boorman.

Potter Occupation.

Florence Suffragist.

Potter Occupation, Miss Boorman. Not offence.

Florence Suffragist. Suffragette. Womanist. Woman. That's what I'm occupied with at the present moment in time and have been for the past sixty years.

Potter Employment.

Florence Suffragette. Sentence seven months.

Potter Can't get enough of it, can you?

Florence I was on marches before you were born.

Potter Which just goes to show how long and ineffectual your campaign has been.

Florence Which division are you putting us in?

Potter Second.

Florence We are politicals. Not thieves or child-killers. We should be placed in first.

Potter (*indicating his form*) Criminal damage. See.

Florence The tide is changing, Potter. Watch out. The water will come rushing in under your feet and you'll find you won't have a pot to piss in. If you insist on placing us in second, you'd better arrange for the prison glazier now. We will immediately proceed to break our windows. It is our legal right to be in first. Visitors we should have, pens, paper. Associated labour. Permitted access to other cells.

    Celia and Eve Douglas enter and join the line.

Potter Nobody's listening. Why don't you give it a rest, Miss Boorman?

Florence Why don't you get yourself a proper job? Instead of collecting birds and putting them in cages. It's more the act of a deranged child than an evolved man, I must warn you. But still I wish you luck.

Potter With what?

Florence You don't have the vote, Potter? No wonder your aspirations are so low. I wish you all the best in the fight for universal suffrage. Any news on Miss Davison?

Potter Name.

Eve Eve Douglas.

Potter Occupation.

Eve Machinist tailor. In Limehouse.

Potter Sentence.

Eve Seven months. Windows.

Potter Name.

Celia You know my name. I know your name.

Potter Name.

Celia Lady Celia Madeline Ottoline Cain.

Potter Occupation.

Celia looks at him, he writes something down. Celia carries some undergarments.

Sentence.

Celia Is there a wardress about, Potter?

No reply.

No matter, you're practically family. An honorary woman by now.

Potter Are you taking me off?

Celia I'm quite serious. I've never been issued undergarments like these before. They've stains in places I don't wish to contemplate. Any chance of some replacement duds? And there wasn't a pair of shoes to be had in the basket so the left one is killing me. I feel like a bloody geisha. Potter? I'm not invisible.

Potter What exactly is it that you want?

Celia What I want is a crêpe-de-chine nightgown and glass slippers. What I'm asking for are undergarments that don't look and smell like someone died in them. Plus two shoes of a similar size. And we would very much like to know how our comrade Emily Wilding Davison is doing. Do you read the papers? She's been unconscious for three days after throwing herself in front of the King's horse. I thought you might have seen the article, even if you only go straight to the sports section.

Potter ignores the request. Celia joins the other women who are assembled in a line waiting for their cell allocation. Potter looks to the Guard.

Potter Get the next lot in.

Celia joins the other women, who are assembled in a line waiting for their cell allocation. Potter continues to write.

Florence How are you feeling now, Mrs Schliefke?

Mrs Schliefke What? I don't suppose we'll have an eyelash left when they're through with us.

Celia It's just about getting used to the frowsy clothes now. Last time we were here Florence tried to steal her hospital slippers when we got out. They weren't even a pair, were they?

Florence I'd formed a bizarre attachment to them. (*To Potter.*) Which just goes to show how quickly one can become institutionalised! Have you visited the zoological gardens, Potter? Do you see what happens to those beasts? They pace up and down. They eat their own tails and faeces. They lose their fur. They make noises in their cages that should only be heard in hell. Their only crime was being rare or beautiful. As is ours, sir. As is ours.

Potter I grant you you're rare, Boorman.

Florence picks up her toothbrush and joins the other women.

Mrs Schliefke One hears it's very healthy to express one's self. It actually prolongs life. I'm rather worried. That I've offended God.

Celia You don't think He's a feminist? I suspect you're right.

Mrs Schliefke It wasn't a very Christian act, was it?

Florence We're smashing up glass, not people.

Mrs Schliefke But still. I can't reconcile it. Turn the other cheek, he said.

Florence You can't very well turn your cheek when you're being held face down in the mud.

Mrs Schliefke I just find it sad. That it's created such a division in the ranks. That discussion couldn't prevail.

Florence You can't discuss something if you're refused a voice, can you?

Mrs Schliefke No. No. Ignore me. I'm too tired to move. No swagger.

Eve Can you get tobacco in here?

Celia You can procure pretty much anything if you've the cash. You did it, then?

Eve What happens in second division?

Florence You're on your own for twenty-three hours of the day. Did you bring a pencil?

Eve No.

Florence breaks the cotton of her petticoat hem, produces a pencil and gives it to Eve without Potter seeing.

Florence Write on the walls. Demand associated labour. And smash your windows if they don't open.

Potter That's enough! You be quiet else you'll go straight to isolation! Now!

Florence I'll be quiet when I die.

Potter Which is what your friend is. Dead.

Florence Dead? When?

Potter Today.

Florence Today. Oh.

A Guard enters.

Mary Nicholson Her skull was smashed in.

Clara Franks It was.

Mrs Schliefke May we go to the chapel, sir, and say a prayer for our sister?

Guard They're ready for them now. Block DX.

Potter You can pray in your cells. Go on then. Piss off.

A Guard leads them away.

SCENE FIVE

Holloway Prison. Night. In various cells in the shadows, women take down their plank beds from the wall and make them up with a blanket. A gas lamp burns in each cell. Briggs does the rounds. She rattles the door of each cell with her keys and shouts; each prisoner must come to the door and reply to her enquiry. Another Wardress sits on their corridor, knitting.

Briggs Alright?

Mrs Schliefke Alright.

At the next cell.

Briggs Alright?

Eve I haven't got a blanket. And can I have the light out, please? I can't turn it down from in here.

At the next cell.

Briggs Alright?

Celia I'm minus a blanket too.

The Wardress unlocks Celia's gate. Then unlocks Eve's.

Briggs Wait. Wait.

The Wardress continues her routine.

Alright?

Florence Alright.

Briggs exits to fetch blankets.

Celia (*to Eve*) They never put the light out.

Eve How long you in for?

Celia Three months. You?

15

Eve Seven.

Celia What do you do?

Eve I'm a machinist. I do collars.

Celia Is it sweated?

Eve They all are. I'd murder for a smoke.

Celia Who would you kill?

Briggs enters with the blankets.

Briggs Shut up, Douglas! Cain. Blanket.

Celia Did anyone ever tell you that you have a wonderful facility for language, Briggs?

Briggs In. Now.

Celia I'm just curious. Do you think you're actually saving time by leaving words out?

Briggs holds the door open for Celia, who walks in. Briggs shuts and locks it, checks that Eve is in her cell, then shuts and locks it.

SCENE SIX

The Prison. Night time. A doctor's office is lit brightly. Dr Vale and Dr Parker set up their equipment. A Nurse lays a white sheet under an armchair. She rearranges it so that it is flat and neat. Dr Vale pours liquid into a jug from a larger one. Dr Parker cleans a long red rubber tube. Dr Vale whistles 'The Man Who Broke the Bank at Monte Carlo'.

Vale Unbearable heat, isn't it?

Parker Stifling.

Vale You've not done this business before, no?

Parker I haven't. Is there anything I should know?

Vale Basic procedure. It's somewhat tougher here than at the asylum. They can be a bit bullish.

The Nurse has finished laying the sheet down.

Nurse Is there anything else you need, Dr Vale?

Vale No, Nurse. You shuffle off home if they let you out.

Nurse Yes, Doctor. Goodbye.

Parker Goodbye, Nurse.

The Nurse exits.

Vale I'm going to the Criterion tonight. Is it any good, do you know?

Parker Underhill said there can be complications. Pneumonia?

Vale Occasionally. Pleurisy's the killer of course. If the liquid goes down the wrong way. Ends up in the lungs. Fatal when it happens. One does entreat them to recant. Up to the eleventh hour they can walk out of here untouched. Stubborn, you see. They're very stubborn. Tomorrow. Don't wear your best suit. Can you put out the light?

Parker turns the gas down and the Doctors exit.

SCENE SEVEN

The Prison kitchen. Morning. Various Suffragettes are on work duty. Celia and Eve peel a vast pile of potatoes together. Once peeled they put them in a huge pot filled with water. Briggs loiters and walks around inspecting the workers.

Eve You don't smoke, do you?

Celia No.

Eve I keep thinking about Miss Davison. Did you know her?

Celia No.

Eve Do you smoke?

Celia No. You just asked me that.

Eve Sorry.

Celia I tried it once. Couldn't get the measure of it.

Eve There's nothing to it. I'll show you one day. Gorgeous, it is. Are you going on strike?

Celia Tomorrow.

Eve You done it before?

Celia Quite a bit. But I've never been pulled in for the feeding.

Eve They sound more like they're being slaughtered than fed.

Celia Yes, it's not very clever.

Eve I keep wondering if she was lonely. When she went out there. Walking out in front of all those crowds. Holding her arm up like that with those great big horses going past her. I hope she didn't regret it at the last moment. It's funny to be part of something. I've never been part of anything before.

Celia It's rather wonderful, isn't it?

Eve Yeah. Besides the actual prison side of it.

Celia Besides the stench. And the noise at night. And the dog soap.

Eve finds dog soap funny.

Eve Dog soap.

Celia Besides that it's rather wonderful.

They laugh. Eve puts a potato in and drops her knife with it. She starts to feel for it.

Lost your knife?

Eve Yeah.

They feel slowly and carefully for the knife; their hands bump into each other's in the vat and they continue to search in the muddied water until Celia produces it.

Celia There.

Eve Ta. I'm a bit scared I'll lose my bottle. If they get me in for the feeding.

Celia There's no shame if you do. Don't be too harsh upon yourself. You're terribly young.

Eve Not really. Beautiful, aren't they? Children.

Celia They are. Do you have any?

Eve No. Not married. You?

Celia Actually I'd prefer not to talk about such things.

Eve Oh.

Celia I'm married to God. I was part of the Poor Clare convent before all of this.

Eve Oh.

Celia I'm a virgin.

Celia smiles at Eve. Celia laughs.

Eve You're not a nun. What's your name?

Briggs Talking! No talking!

Celia Celia. May I call you by your first name?

Eve Eve. As in the garden.

They smile. Silence. They keep peeling the potatoes.

SCENE EIGHT

*The House of Commons. Afternoon. Question Time.
Keir Hardie addresses the Prime Minister, Herbert
Asquith. The Speaker presides. Members of Parliament
make the usual white noise.*

Speaker Pray silence for the Honourable Member for
Merthyr Tydfil, Keir Hardie.

Hardie Prime Minister, when will you put a stop to the
forcible feeding of the militant section of the women's
suffrage movement in Holloway Prison?

*The usual Question Time cacophony that sounds
vaguely like a farmyard and has a flavour of derision
to it.*

Asquith We are simply keeping these women alive.
Should this hospital treatment stop they would starve
and we have no desire for any more suffragette martyrs.

Hardie Might I remind the Honourable Gentlemen of the
House that the last death connected to a hunger strike
was in 1870. And the prisoner in question died not from
the fasting but as a result of the forcible feeding. These
women are political prisoners. What they are being
subjected to is an illegal process. They are worn and
weak with hunger. In this condition they are seized upon
and held down by anything up to ten persons. Are you
aware, sir, that a steel gag is often enforced? It is lodged
between their teeth to keep their mouth open?

An MP I would have thought the primary objective would be to keep those women's mouths shut!

A loud guffaw from the others.

Speaker Order! Order!

Hardie I have enquired before under what law this feeding was done, but Mr Masterman was unable to say without notice. Only that it was by order of the Home Office. My understanding was that this enforcement was for those certified to be insane.

An MP Quite right! Bloody madwomen!

More guffaws.

Hardie If women die from this the blood is on your hands, Prime Minister. Might I say the behaviour of the House today and on days previous to this when I have asked this question has been deeply shocking and repugnant. Had I not heard the laughter myself I could not have believed that a body of gentlemen could have found reason for mirth and applause in a scene which I venture to say has no parallel in the recent history of our country.

An MP Go home to your washing!

An MP Home to your washing! Home to your washing!

Guffaws.

Speaker Order! Order!

Hardie I put it to you, sir, their lives are in your hands. Shame on our society for letting this happen. Let British men think over this spectacle.

Asquith I can only repeat that these women are in Holloway of their own volition. And their refusal to eat is at their own behest.

'Hear, hear!'s from the benches.

Speaker I believe there was a pressing question about taxation from the bench?

SCENE NINE

Holloway Prison. Evening. Women lie on their beds or sit on the floors in their cells.

Celia sits in her cell, reading; she wears glasses. Briggs unlocks the door and enters.

Briggs I didn't know you wore spectacles, Lady Cain.

Celia Yes. I try to use them sparingly. I think they're rather unbecoming.

Briggs Literary. Very nice.

Celia Thank you, Briggs. Was there . . . something?

Briggs Your husband, miss.

Celia Yes? What about him?

Briggs He's here, miss. To see you.

Celia Here? My husband?

Briggs Yes, miss. Excuse me.

Briggs leaves the cell and William Cain enters. He has a bottle of wine, newspapers, a cake and some flowers.

William Celia.

Celia goes to him and kisses his cheek, takes the flowers.

Celia Will?

William Yes. Sorry if it's a . . . I was going to give you some notice and come next week but I thought unannounced might be pleasant.

Celia Yes. Quite. So . . . Are these for me?

William No. They're for the psychopath on the next floor.

Celia It's so sweet of you. Sorry. I'm a bit . . .

William What?

Celia It's just a shock.

William Yes.

Celia Was it difficult to get in?

William I robbed the firm. And a bank.

Celia Yes.

Pause.

William Pinson got me in. The old reptile.

Celia You've brought everything.

Celia scours the front page of a newspaper. Reads:

'Our Prime Minister cannot be blamed for not wanting to give women the vote when it would be in the hands of such hysterics.' Cowards.

William Journalists. Politicians. What do you expect? Drink?

Celia I can't believe you're here.

William You always said I was terribly predictable. Bertram wants to get married.

Celia He told me. Said I was to soften you up about it.

William pours some wine into the mug and raises it to Celia.

William Cheers. (*Taking in the cell.*) Smaller than I imagined.

Celia Did anyone see you come in?

William I didn't climb over the turret. You mean your sisters in arms? You're worried they'll think you're spoilt.

Celia I mustn't have unfair advantages. Access. It's not fair. Do you see?

William I do. I'm a rather brilliant lawyer, not a child. Strange to be in the crucible itself.

Pause.

Celia It feels like a rather private activity.

William You seem more yourself in here than at home.

Celia Really? I can't get used to this at all.

William Do you want me to leave?

Celia No, of course not.

William So what do you think about the two of them?

Celia Bertie seems pretty smitten.

William Her father's a bit of a climber.

Celia As long as they're happy.

William That's enough, do you think?

Celia Don't become middle-aged, Will. Please. I've never asked you for anything.

William walks over to the window and looks out.

William You're very high up, aren't you? One would need a dozen sheets to shimmy down. Those bloody great walls. Christ. (*Pause.*) What?

Celia Nothing.

William sits next to Celia who takes his hand.

So . . . tell me what's happening in the outside world?

William Nothing. Nothing's happening. How is it in here? Any changes?

William looks away distracted, Celia looks at the newspaper.

Celia No. Christ. There's a warning here to telephone girls. Says to be careful about receiving bouquets as men have been drugging them.

William sees Celia's prison books.

William You've some books?

Celia No. They've built a cairn over Captain Scott's grave. Where his tent was.

William Sorry?

Celia They've put a cross on top and planted his skis upright in the ice next to it. It looks strangely religious in the middle of nowhere.

William They were only eleven miles off. One more day and they'd have made it. I think you should see a doctor. When you're released.

Celia Why?

William A psychiatrist.

Celia Do you think I'm mental?

William Not at all. People simply go to Klein for advice. I expect one day it'll be all the rage.

Celia Klein? You've found someone already.

William He was recommended.

Celia So who have you been talking to about your lunatic wife?

William Nobody. Langham was saying his brother's been having treatment since he came back from the Transvaal.

Celia Treatment?

William If nothing else it might be good material for your stories. I want you to be happier is all. It's my birthday.

Celia What? Oh God, Will, I'm sorry. All the days meld into one here.

William You did ask me for something. When you were ten years old. You asked to borrow some of my clothes. So that you could adopt a disguise. And you begged me to run away with you. To Egypt.

Celia Ah. Yes. Well. I was a child then. Everything seemed possible.

William Yes. You were a child. So was I.

SCENE TEN

Hyde Park. Afternoon. Some soapboxes: Florence stands on one. Fellow Suffragettes are near her, including Mrs Schliefke, who presides over the singing. A small crowd has gathered to listen, including Charlie Power, Hunt and Brown.

Florence Over a thousand women have been to prison during the course of this agitation. Last summer there were one hundred and two suffragettes incarcerated at one time. Of these ninety were forcibly fed. Some of them twice a day. Our comrade Kitty Marion has been force-fed up to two hundred times to date. The last horrors we witnessed were those of the Boer War. Women and children starved and died in concentration camps that British soldiers erected and imposed upon them. We shouted then about the outrage and we were heard. We are in peacetime now. Violence is being inflicted behind secret walls. Upon neither spies nor even wives of our enemies. But upon our own women.

Celia and Eve join the women. Celia and Eve light up cigarettes.

Hunt How dare you, madam? How dare you compare yourselves to our men who fought out there!

Florence I was not, sir. But we are soldiers of a sort.

Hunt Men gave their lives! They died that this country might prosper and that you might be secure!

Florence My point was that no one should be hidden, gagged or muzzled whether it be in a police cell, a prison or a refugee camp.

Brown Unnatural they are! And look at that. Smoking in one of the royal parks. If you was my dog!

Celia Are you addressing me, sir?

Florence Let it never be said that we did not know what was going on around us. Or that we knew but did not fight to change it.

Brown Christ. In a minute. Not now but in a minute . . . if you was my dog!

Celia I'm very glad I'm not your dog.

Florence We have been prevented recently from petitioning Parliament. It is every citizen's right to do so. The present Liberal government forces us to be militant! Deeds not words!

Brown I'd do you a deed. I'd do you all a bloody deed.

Celia Do you have healthy relations with your wife, sir?

Brown You bitch! Anarchist socialist bitch!

Hunt Language, sir! This is a public place. And the ladies!

Brown explodes and heads over to Celia to try and hit her.

Brown I'll give them fucking ladies. That's what you want, isn't it, you bitch! Bitches! Unnatural fucking bitches, all of you!

Charlie Power intervenes and tries to keep Brown from Celia.

Charlie Oi! Back off now! Get out of it!

Brown A right fucking servicing is what they want!

Hunt Sir! Stop this now! Stand back!

Florence Sir! Celia! Celia!

There is a messy scuffle. Brown is floored by Charlie.

Charlie Had enough yet, eh?

Brown gets up and runs off.

Brown Piss off, the lot of you!

Hunt We should find a policeman.

Florence You are naive, sir, if you think they'll be helpful to us. No surrender!

Women No surrender!

Charlie (*to Celia*) Do you want a brandy? Shall I get you one?

Celia What? A what?

Charlie For the shock. I work over there at the Ritz.

Celia Thank you, but there's no harm done.

Charlie Sorry about that, ladies. Come over and find me sometime. I'll serve you the best wine and only charge you for house.

Florence Thank you, sir. And good luck to you with getting the vote. No surrender!

Charlie No surrender!

Charlie runs off, amused. Florence goes to her pile of pamphlets and starts to give them out. Eve takes Celia's arm.

Eve Celia.

Celia You kept very quiet.

Eve I didn't know what to . . . I didn't want to . . .

Celia What? Show any vestige of backbone? Come on, let's get a stiff drink.

Celia and Eve leave. Florence watches them. Mrs Schliefke takes the cue for the women to start singing 'The March of the Women'. They sing a few lines from it.

SCENE ELEVEN

Holloway Prison. Eve's cell. Night. A lamp with a gas jet burns in the dark. Eve sits, motionless, on a plank bed. She lies down and tries to settle away from the light. She gets up and goes to the grille in the door. Day five of her strike.

Eve Excuse me. Excuse me!

The sound of footsteps and keys. The Wardress stands outside the cell.

Can you put out the light? I can't sleep with it on.

Wardress You're under observation.

Eve For what?

The Wardress walks away.

For what?

Eve lies on the bed and watches the gas jet, then turns away from it. The flame flickers, Eve sits up. It becomes brighter. She walks to the door.

I can't have the light on! Please! Please!

Eve picks up her shoe from the floor and smashes the glass lamp. A bell sounds. The Wardress and a Guard come in and drag her out of her cell.

SCENE TWELVE

Dr Klein's surgery. Afternoon. Dr Klein sits opposite Celia Cain. Occasionally he refers to notes about her on his desk.

Klein You haven't been sleeping?

Celia No.

Klein Your husband is very worried.

Celia glances at the book on Klein's desk.

It's about Elizabeth the First.

Klein finds the frontispiece with Elizabeth's words. He gives it back to her, Celia reads it.

Celia 'I freeze and yet am burned.'

Klein Do you like history?

Celia It depends whose it is.

Celia refers to her file.

How much of mine is in there?

Klein In your file? You grew up in Hampshire. Married at eighteen. From a large family, your father served in India, your mother lives in Maidenhead.

Celia File is an anagram of life, isn't it? You're an alienist, aren't you? So what would your verdict be to the court so far? That I'm too sane to be locked up or too mad to let roam?

Klein I'm sure you're quite *compos mentis*. But Holloway must take its toll, no?

Celia I've led a privileged life. Prison redresses the balance rather. What else is in there?

Klein You had your first child when you were nineteen. The first of seven.

Celia I don't want to talk about my children.

Klein Why not?

Celia Because they're mine. What do you think of Freud?

Klein I find his attitude towards women is both patronising and irresponsible. You were placed in the hospital ward the last time you were incarcerated?

Celia My window looked out onto the girls in the exercise yard. Two of them were always laughing together. One was about eighteen the other perhaps thirty. The girl's hair kept blowing into her face and eyes and her companion kept brushing it away for her because the girl needed to keep her hands warm in her pockets. The friend understood that.

Klein Is that what you would like? To be understood?

Celia To be loved, you mean?

Klein Is that your definition of understanding?

Celia What I would really like is . . . is a cigarette.

Klein Do you understand your husband?

Celia I'm not supposed to. I'm his wife. We grew up together. I adored him from age eight to eleven. So I suppose we had three good years.

Klein Your husband would like for you to be exempt from conviction if you are ever part of a Suffragette Deputation again.

Celia I'm always part of the Deputation. And if you're part of it then the whole point is to get yourself arrested.

Klein You petition at Parliament?

Celia We endeavour to. And Downing Street.

Klein In which case you'll be arraigned next week. If I pronounce your mind fragile the court will be reluctant to pass sentence, do you see?

Celia And you've discussed this with my husband?

Klein It was more his idea than mine, in point of fact.

Celia So he's not actually worried about my mental health. Just that I shouldn't be incarcerated.

Klein He is concerned that your health will deteriorate inside.

Celia What else?

Klein Nothing else. I'm hoping that you will walk free on Wednesday in which case we should meet on a weekly basis. On a good day I'm terribly perceptive.

Celia And on a bad day?

Klein Nobody sees me on a bad day.

Celia I like this area. Have you practised here long?

Klein The Jews have a very high opinion of themselves.

Celia I'm sorry?

Klein It's a very Jewish area.

Celia You're Jewish, aren't you?

Klein German. I thought about anglicising my name because people often jump to the wrong conclusion.

Celia Except then you'd be Dr Little?

Klein Quite. So. I ask myself, what can we do for this new woman we see before us?

Celia Very little I expect. Goodbye, Klein. I'll see myself out.

Celia stands and exits.

SCENE THIRTEEN

Celia's parlour. Celia and Florence have a pile of leaflets and letters to collate and put into envelopes. Florence is a mini-production line. Celia is slow and stops now to smoke.

Florence You're very distracted today.

Celia I'm going to the prison later. To visit Miss Douglas.

Florence stops and looks at her.

What?

Florence resumes work.

Flo?

Florence I said nothing.

Celia You don't need to.

Florence There are people inside at the moment who you've known a lot longer than that one.

Celia Why do you dislike her?

Florence I don't. You became very close. Very quickly.

Celia I don't think she has many chums.

Florence Where did you put the list and pencil?

Celia vaguely looks for the list and pencil.

33

Celia She's managed to get herself arrested every time. That's pretty impressive. And she only joined the Union a few months ago.

Florence She should have signed up a lot sooner then, shouldn't she?

Celia She's had no advantages. No education to speak of.

Florence She's not the only factory girl locked up in there. You behave like schoolgirls together. Giggling. Smoking. Always setting up your own little camp at meetings. I don't like people attaching themselves to the cause just because they have nothing else. We're not a headquarters for lost souls.

Celia I'd have thought that was exactly what we were. And I don't call serving seven months' hard labour attaching yourself to the cause. It's hardly the action of a sycophant, is it? What do you want her to do? Nail herself up to the cell wall?

Florence Exactly.

Celia What?

Florence A martyr. She's lonely. And she plays the victim.

Celia She doesn't. Anyway, isn't that the point? That women are victims.

Florence No no no! I can't believe you sometimes.

Celia By our circumstances. I didn't mean victims per se. It's just a word, Florence. Don't react to me like I'm Lord Curzon or the bloody sledgehammer. It's just phraseology. For God's sake, we're both on the same side, aren't we?

Florence She's become addicted to the drama of it all. I tried telling her the history of the movement and she asked me if I'd met any of the famous actresses.

Celia Which is an innocent enough question.

Florence It's not the point though, is it? Why we're here.

Celia You're being very extreme.

Florence Well let's not be extreme, then. Let's not care who's part of the Union or why they've joined. Let's just have a party and sing militant songs, shall we? What the hell are we going to achieve if we're not extreme? And are you ever going to stop smoking that bloody cigarette and help me here?

Celia I'm helping you already. You work faster when you're angry. (*Pause.*) I tell you what, Flo, if things continue to flag here they're dying for you to become part of the Russian Women's Army.

Florence The Battalion of Death? They sound a bit soft.

Celia starts to help.

Oh. She moves.

The women work together.

SCENE FOURTEEN

Holloway Prison. Eve's cell. Dusk. Celia is in civilian clothes; she has a basket of provisions. Eve is in her prison uniform.

Eve I didn't think they let people in.

Celia I'm not people.

Eve Did you have to pay?

Celia No. I walked though the walls. How have you been? I just wondered if there was anything I could do for you out there? Or bring you?

35

Eve I don't want anything. Why have you come to see me?

Celia You're striking. What day are you on?

Eve Three.

Celia I thought you might want me to take a message to your sister. In Limehouse.

Eve No. Thanks.

Celia takes out parcels from her basket.

Celia I brought you some spring water. And look, so you don't have to use the dog soap. Lemon. Smell.

Eve smells it.

How's your stomach? . . . You'll be out in a month. I miss our working in the kitchen. Those mountains of potatoes. Perverse, isn't it? You're tired. I should let you rest.

Celia leaves the basket for Eve on the floor and prepares to leave.

Eve There's a girl in your cell now. She's fifteen. She didn't stop screaming all night.

Celia You've had no sleep, poor thing. What's she in for?

Eve She smothered her child. They were going to hang her or send her to the asylum. Except her employer has offered to buy her back. He's been raping her since she was eleven. They kicked her out when she started to show and she had the baby months before its time in an alleyway.

Celia Oh. Well, perhaps they won't let him take her back.

Eve They'll let him. Money. Bastard.

Celia Did you ever negotiate them turning out the light for you? There's lavender there too. And newspapers.

And pen and paper. Have you met anyone new? Have you had any nice chats in the kitchen?

Eve Who else are you visiting? Celia?

Celia Nobody. I'm not visiting anybody else.

Eve Why not?

Celia Oh, and books. So you don't have to read prison issue.

Eve Celia.

Celia Yes? . . . My father always said it was a lie if you didn't finish your sentence.

Eve It wasn't a lie.

Celia No.

Eve No. It wasn't a fucking lie.

Celia picks up a prison-issue book.

Celia I wasn't being especially literal. You haven't touched your *How to Maintain a Perfect Household*. Some of the pages aren't even cut.

Eve You laughed. When we were smashing all those windows.

Celia sits herself next to Eve and looks at the book.

Celia Yes.

Eve I've been . . .

Celia What? What have you been? The only really important thing is to be brave. (*Reading the book.*) 'How to remove stubborn stains.'

Celia turns the pages.

Not one wretched sinner has been interested in reading about shining steps or baking the perfect cake.

Eve I'm glad.

Celia That no one wanted to bake to perfection?

Eve That you only came to see me.

Their heads become closer, they turn the pages together.

Celia Yes. Yes, so am I.

They gently move against each other, Eve touches Celia's face, they kiss, gently. Eve breaks away; self-conscious of her breath, she covers her mouth. Celia uncovers it and pulls her back to her. They kiss more strongly. Celia drops the book.

SCENE FIFTEEN

The Cains' parlour. Evening. Celia sits in the dark by a lamp. William walks in, puts down his bag and takes off his gloves. Mrs Collins tends the fire.

William Evening, Mrs Collins.

Mrs Collins Sir. Weather's on the turn.

William It is. (*To Celia.*) How was your day?

Celia It was alright. You look terribly serious.

William I need to ask you something.

Celia Is it to do with your mother?

William No. Nothing to do with Mo. That'll be fine, thank you, Mrs Collins.

Mrs Collins Very good, sir.

Mrs Collins exits. Pause.

Celia What is it?

William How was your work? Did you finish your story?

Celia No. I'm never going to finish it before the next stretch. Florence has gone in again, did I tell you already?

William No.

Celia I forget who I've spoken to. For that policeman in Cannon Street. Five months they gave her when it should be three maximum.

William Really?

Celia She's making a huge stink about the feeding. She's holed herself up with furniture and refuses to come out. She's never done that before.

William And you haven't changed your mind? About the Deputation next month? Or striking in there?

Celia Why would I? Have you been at the Club? Maybe Pinson could put in a word for Flo?

William I'll ask him. Although I suspect she'd rather I didn't.

Celia You're not squiffy already, are you?

William Would you just stop all of this please, Celia? For me.

Celia Stop?

William I don't ask it lightly.

Pause.

Celia You said you'd never ask me to.

William That was before it was dangerous.

Celia First of all you try and pronounce me lunatic. Now you want me to be a no-show.

William Better a no-show than a dead one, don't you think? Who do you actually think you represent?

Celia Half the human race.

William I don't see my mother begging you to lay down your life for her.

Celia I don't think she'd be averse to it.

William You don't represent the whole of womankind.

Celia Because they're institutionalised. Women are prisoners in their own home. They don't even realise it.

William But you do? Thanks.

Celia looks at him. Pause.

I've not asked you to step down before. I've not interfered. In fifteen years. Would you? Please? For me? . . . I see.

Celia Actually you don't. I know when you changed. It was Hyde Park last summer. Ever since then you've tried to accept it but you can't.

William What? What about Hyde Park?

Celia The march. When you saw all our thousands converge. Men don't like to see a convoy of women. It unsexes us.

William Ridiculous.

Celia You're white with anger underneath all your apparent support, aren't you?

William Am I really? I'm going out. Is that permitted? Or is that also up for analysis?

Celia That's all you ever do really, isn't it? Go out. Come home. I suppose there's a routine to it. You leave sober and you return plastered.

William Did you ever think why that might be? Do you know how many evenings you spend furthering the cause?

Celia How many hours do you spend at the law firm?

William As many as I need to in order to support my family.

Celia And getting tight at the Club is another act of altruistic charity you perform for us, is it?

William I go to the Club that I might hear myself think.

Celia Are your blotto thoughts more coherent than your sober ones? Or is it just that they are louder?

William Louder. Stronger. Purer. Funnier. You haven't the slightest inkling of what goes on inside my head. You treat me as though I were stupid.

Celia Well, I don't, actually. I just don't.

William And then you use that tone. That you use at the meetings.

Celia You're acting like a child.

William Why wouldn't I? You preferred me as a child.

William starts to leave.

Celia No, don't walk out. I know you're furious. But we're talking. And we never do. Talk.

William It's rather louder than talk. And I'm not angry. I'm simply tired. Very tired. Don't wait up. You're quite sure about all this? You won't change your mind?

Celia Don't come into my room late. Pissed.

William I haven't done that in a long time. Even animals know when they're not wanted.

William exits.

SCENE SIXTEEN

Holloway. Night time. Florence is in her cell. There are a table and chair barricaded against the door. Guards and Wardresses stand outside. One Guard holds a long rubber hose pipe. Another Guard waits near a faucet.

Guard You're keeping the doctors waiting.

Florence Good. Better for them to wait than to dishonour their profession.

Guard You still refuse to come with us?

Florence I do.

Guard That's prison property you're using. We're coming in.

They start to push the cell door against the barricade of the table and chair. Florence tries to keep the table in place.

Florence I'm a political prisoner, not a lunatic! 'Only be thou brave and . . . only be thou brave . . .'

Guard In!

They force the door in against the table. Florence struggles with them and runs into a corner. The Guards take Florence from her cell into a punishment cell. There is a mess of struggle and people.

Do it, Moyle. Everyone else out!

A Guard comes in with the hose and directs it at Florence. She screams with the pressure and the cold of it, huddles into a ball. The hose is kept on far longer than is needed. Finally Moyle turns it away and another Guard turns it off at the faucet. Florence is disorientated, crying. The Guards haul her up and lead her out of the cell towards the Doctor's office.

42

Eve's lodgings. Afternoon. Celia and Eve are on Eve's bed, semi-clothed. There are a couple of empty bottles of beer. Eve has her head on Celia's lap. The sun streams onto the floor.

Celia We should go to France. You'd adore the Parisian women. They've got the most amazing breasts. What?

Eve I don't want to be around loads of women.

Celia I wasn't inferring that you were a raving bulldyke. Just that they were lovely. I'm going to buy you a rug. We can lie on it together. Sunbathe. On your floor.

Eve Don't buy me anything. I don't need anything.

Celia I'm not lying there as it is.

Eve I swept it. This morning.

Celia Doesn't stop you getting splinters in your arse, does it?

Eve Put a blanket down.

Celia I could have it delivered. And be wrapped up inside it?

Eve What?

Celia Nothing. I'll get you one. Is there any more beer?

Eve I'll get some.

Eve starts to get up, Celia stops her.

Celia Would you like a Persian one? Like a flying carpet?

Eve I don't want a fucking rug. What?

Celia When you swear. I like it.

43

Eve Fucking rug. Fucking Persian fucking woven fucking carpets.

Celia kisses Eve. They embrace.

Eve It's a bit . . . terrifying.

Celia It's not. I promise you it's not.

Eve I just never thought . . . it's like I've been . . .

Celia Waiting.

Eve I wish that I was untouched.

Celia Nobody really touched you.

Eve I'd like to be . . . clean. For you.

Celia I think I love you.

Eve looks away, moves away.

Eve? Eve.

Eve shakes her head.

Darling. Do you want me to go?

Eve shakes her head.

What then? Please.

Eve It's just . . . good. That's good. That you . . .

Celia That I love you.

Eve nods her head, cries.

Eve I wish I was . . .

Celia What? What, sweetheart?

Eve I wish I was a virgin who read books.

Eve cries and Celia laughs. Celia holds her.

Celia Angel. Promise me you'll never be a virgin. Especially a bookish one. It's alright. You cry, sweetheart. You cry. I don't want you to be anything. You hear me? Nothing other than what you are. Please.

Eve Yes.

Celia Don't be anything. Just be as you are.

Celia kisses Eve.

Eve Yes.

Celia That is all that I want.

Eve All I want.

Celia All I want.

Blackout.

End of Act One.

Act Two

SCENE ONE

Epping Forest. Dusk. Eve sits on a tree stump and smokes a cigarette. Celia Cain approaches with a large rifle in hand, pointed at Eve. Eve looks at her.

Celia Smoking. In a public place.

There are several gunshots in the vicinity. Eve looks around at the woods and smiles.

Eve Are you going to shoot me?

Celia I might tie you to a tree. Why aren't you joining in like a good scout?

Eve There weren't enough to go around.

Celia Bloody feeding frenzy. They act like children. Someone'll get fed up with it in a minute. Probably Schliefke. What's the matter?

Eve Just our pretending. Being distant.

Celia Distance can be very alluring.

Celia kisses Eve but breaks from her as she sees women approach: Florence, Mrs Schliefke and other Suffragettes, all with revolvers in hand.

Florence Celia, Miss Douglas, are you with us?

Celia Evidently we are, Flo, else we wouldn't be stood in the middle of Epping Forest, would we?

Florence Miss Beecham, would you lend your revolver to Miss Douglas, please? Let's try for the trees over there. And remember. Cock.

Two of the women giggle. Miss Beecham gives her revolver to Eve.

Ladies. Please.

Suffragette Sorry.

Second Suffragette Sorry.

The women arrange themselves to shoot.

Florence Come then. Pick your targets.

The women aim.

Mrs Schliefke I'm still rather perplexed why Lady Cain has a rifle and we all have revolvers.

Celia Do you want it?

Mrs Schliefke No no. I was merely commenting.

The women aim again silently, carefully. Their attention melds the group into one serious whole.

Florence Now. Fire!

The women shoot in unison.

Good. And again.

They cock and aim their guns.

Fire!

They fire.

Ready . . .

They cock their guns.

Aim.

They aim.

Fire.

They fire.

Good.

Mrs Schliefke Should we not be practising our throwing, Miss Boorman? For tomorrow.

Celia If you can't hit a window at two feet you shouldn't really be on it, Mrs Schliefke.

Mrs Schliefke I'm not saying I can't. Simply that it might be fruitful to rehearse. All I meant about the rifle was that we won't really ever use it, will we?

Florence Preparation is all.

Mrs Schliefke Quite. But my point is . . .

Celia Do you want my big gun, Mrs Schliefke? I give it to you. Here.

Celia takes off her rifle and presents it to Mrs Schliefke, who will not take it.

Mrs Schliefke I don't want it. And actually I rather resent your tone. We're all on the same side after all, aren't we?

Celia Absolutely. It doesn't mean we cease to be individuals though, does it?

Florence takes the rifle.

Florence We've no time for this. Let's get back to the targets . . . Celia?

Celia We'll catch you up.

Florence hesitates.

What? I thought we were snipers, not schoolgirls.

The other women start to walk away, leaving Florence.

Florence It's messy. To divide up like this.

Celia Schliefke says you're on Downing Street next week.

Florence You need to get on with her better.

Celia Why did I hear it from her and not you?

Florence I thought I'd told you.

Celia That's utter rot. You don't listen to a word I say, do you? You need to give your body time to recover.

Florence There is no time, Celia. If we don't keep pushing.

Celia There are thousands have been in and willing to go in again. Your dead bones are good for no one except your dog, Flo. And I'm not looking after that stinking hound if you don't come out alive.

Florence Are you coming?

Celia You're not twenty-one.

Florence And I have no desire to be such an age. All I remember of being twenty-one was crying like a loon. We're lining up the cans now.

Florence walks away.

Eve Does Florence know?

Celia Flo's omniscient. She knows everything.

Eve Do you mind that she knows?

Celia Why would I?

Celia takes Eve's face in her hands, looks at her.

SCENE TWO

A Gentleman's Club. Evening. Grey sits with Seely at one table. Curzon, drunk, sits at another with Cecil. William Cain sits by himself. Men drink, smoke, read the news.

Grey What are you working out?

Seely Controversial Russian composer. Ten letters.

Grey I thought they were all controversial.

Seely Fourth letter 'a'.

Grey What? Why?

Seely Rivers brought it back for me. From America. It's a puzzle. Word-cross.

Grey Word what?

Seely You fill in the white squares and the words going down have to tally with the across letters and words too, do you see?

Seely hands it to Grey.

Grey Bloody stupid. Child's game, surely?

Seely The Yanks are going ga-ga about it.

Grey We've produced a race of bloody infants.

Curzon Stravinsky.

Seely Thank you.

Grey Didn't have you down as a bohemian, Curzon.

Curzon How's that burgundy, Cain?

William It's good.

Curzon And how is your wife?

The other men look towards William and Curzon.

William Quite well.

Curzon Hasn't lost her appetite lately?

William ignores the remark. Curzon pours himself another drink.

Cecil I think you might have had enough, old chap?

Curzon Is the little lady inside or outside at the moment, Cain?

William Where my wife is at this moment is no business of yours, sir.

Curzon Quite. Possibly it's rather difficult to ascertain her whereabouts most of the time?

William Why do you talk out the notion of female suffrage every time it comes up in the House?

Grey I wasn't aware that we did.

William What are you actually scared of?

Grey I'm sorry?

William The first time it was proposed you prioritised a lighting bill. You debated the pros and cons of automobile lamps for hours to prevent any debate about the rights of women.

Curzon Road safety, Cain. Damn important.

William You've torpedoed their bills ever since.

Grey It's not strictly a political matter.

William Then what is it?

Grey Logistics.

William Do you imagine you'll be mentally castrated if you give them a voice?

Curzon Curious that the term should come to you so easily, don't you think? Castrated, what?

Cecil Steady on, Curzon.

Seely Actually I don't think many of our cabinet would notice mental castration. It's more the noise in their private rooms they'd object to.

William And what's your thinking on it?

Seely I prefer to do my thinking at work, not here.

William The last time my wife was in Holloway a woman in the next door cell was heavily pregnant. She finally gave birth. In her cell. In the middle of the night. She had a child.

Curzon What did you expect her to have, a monkey?

William What are you? A man or a puppet?

Curzon You'd know how it feels to be a puppet with a wife like yours, no?

William If you insult my wife once more I shall cuff you.

Curzon If you so much as brush my collar I'll make it my business to have you ejected from Chambers. Chancery. And anywhere you desire to frequent.

Seely Come on, chaps. We're not a load of navvies.

A Waiter approaches with another bottle of wine for William.

Put Mr Cain's bill on our tab, would you?

William No.

William stands and prepares to leave.

Curzon Go on, Cain. Save your money and spend it on your wife. Buy her a square meal. Or a gag.

William approaches Curzon, pulls him and punches him. Curzon reels and falls, covering his head.

Not my head! Please. Please. Not my head.

The gentlemen watch as Cecil goes to Curzon's side and William leaves.

William Go back to your washing, Curzon! Go back to your fucking washing!

SCENE THREE

The Prison. Florence's cell. Night. Briggs stands at the door.

Florence Why does he want to see me?

Briggs does not reply.

Are you silent because you're not interested or is it a tactic to terrify me?

Briggs Trouble.

Florence nods. Dr Vale comes in with notes in his hand.

Vale Miss Boorman.

Florence Yes.

Vale Dr Vale.

Florence I know who you are. How many unwilling mouths did you feed today?

Vale It's my day off, actually.

Pause. Vale looks at the walls of the cell.

Did you write this? It's from the Bible.

Florence It's for those who come in after me. To lift their spirits. This is a strange way for you to spend your time off.

Vale It's been bothering me. The treatment. Usually with new procedure one becomes easier with it as time goes on. This time I've felt the reverse. To see women emaciated. Terrified.

Florence You should write to the papers. Tell them how it is.

Vale I'm a general practitioner, not a journalist. And there's been more than enough of all that.

Florence So what do you want with me? This isn't a confessional box.

Vale They said I might speak to you.

Florence And you've spoken.

Dr Vale sits down.

Did you wish to become a doctor when you were a child?

Vale It was expected of me. Yes. I did want to. How is your mouth?

Florence I can speak. That's all that matters to me.

Vale You lost three teeth. The last time you underwent forcible feeding.

Florence I did not lose them, sir. They were not mislaid. They were smashed. By the steel gag that they used to force my mouth open.

Vale Any pain since?

Florence None to speak of.

Dr Vale stands up, walks to the window.

Vale Some of your women on the outside attacked one of our doctors, you know? In an alleyway. Last week, on his way home from here. They whipped him with a riding crop. What do you say to that?

Florence I hope he paid them the going rate.

Vale My wife has no sympathy with the movement.

Florence Would you like me to visit her when I'm out? Is that what this is about?

Vale You have influence here. You're the most senior suffragette who goes on strike.

Florence Yes.

Vale Your people planted another bomb in a railway station. They burn down houses. I can't see why you've reverted to such low tactics when you were starting to gain ground.

Florence We've been gaining ground for years. It becomes more tiring than encouraging in the end. One step forward, two steps back. We ask for very little. Simply to be represented. Taxation without representation amounts to tyranny, don't you think?

Vale How is your heart?

Florence Are you asking me if I'm in love?

Vale If it's weak you must abstain from striking.

No reply.

You're shouted at. Spat upon. Subjected to violence. Why do you do it?

Florence It's what I call life, Doctor. Life.

Vale The younger girls. Some of them will not be able to bear children if they continue to abuse their bodies in this way.

Florence We all have to make sacrifices.

Vale But theirs may be larger than yours.

Florence That is their choice.

Vale Your sister died whilst you were serving time here last autumn. You asked to go to both her sickbed and funeral. You were denied both appeals. That must have been harsh. You were teachers in the same school, weren't you?

Florence finds it hard to speak.

Florence Don't.

Vale Don't . . . what?

Florence I prefer not to.

Vale I've upset you? I'm sorry.

Florence I want to be alone now.

Vale Consider. What I've said to you. Will you?

Florence No. The doctor before you said he would make a mental and physical wreck of me if I continued to strike. Is that humane?

Vale I've given you my time. My care. I'm sorry that you won't listen.

Vale leaves.

Florence (*to herself*) 'Only be thou strong and very courageous. Only be thou strong and very courageous.'

SCENE FOUR

A park at night. Celia and Eve are up against a back wall, kissing. They are in a hidden spot but are still vaguely on guard against passers by. Still they are more involved with each other than anything else. The sound of a police bell. Celia breaks away. They sit on a bench together. Eve rolls a cigarette, she breathes deep. Celia smiles at her.

Celia Cold?

Eve No.

Celia Good.

Eve What?

Celia laughs.

What?

Celia shakes her head. They look at each other and smile and it becomes a laugh. Eve kisses Celia. They are both aware of the danger but can't stop. A dog barks. They part slowly.

Eve Dog. There's foxes behind my block. You got foxes near you?

Celia No.

Eve I listen to them at night. They always sound like they're in such fucking pain when they're doing it. I used to cry. Listening to them. The other night I didn't. First time.

Celia Will you make me one?

Eve I'll get you a cigarette case. Then you'll always have some in reserve.

Eve gives Celia her cigarette. Celia tries to light it, fails. Eve cups her hands around the light, Celia cups her hands, the cigarette doesn't light, they start to kiss each other's hands and mouth, the cigarette forgotten.

Celia Thank you.

Eve I keep thinking I'll try to be more restrained when I see you next. Sophisticated. But I never am.

Celia I wouldn't want you to be.

Celia takes Eve's hand. Eve takes Celia's hand with both of her hands. Celia takes her hand away and puts it under Eve's skirts.

Is that sophisticated?

Eve It's beautiful. Beautiful.

Celia Good.

>   *They laugh. They kiss gently then sit with their heads together.*

Eve Do you see the really bright one?

Celia It's Venus. Ishtar.

Eve I keep thinking about your body. I'll be walking down the street or stacking shelves and I'm smiling like a bloody madwoman. People think I've been turned by prison. I make noises and I don't know I'm doing it. I'm mentally stripping you all the time. I never wanted to see anyone's body before.

Celia Not even Mr Blair's?

Eve Don't joke about that.

Celia Can you roll me a thinner cigarette please, sweet?

Eve He always wanted the lamp turned up full. He said he wanted to see the things I was doing to him and that I should see them too.

Celia Bastard.

Eve My fault. Should have got out.

Celia You were fifteen.

Eve Old enough. I wasn't a child. I felt nausea. Just the sight of his shoulders, fat fucking freckled shoulders.

>   *Celia takes her hand away from Eve's petticoats. Eve takes Celia's hand.*

I never thought I minded about all of that. No broken bones. No baby. Since I've known you I've minded. A lot.

Celia You're perfect. You're not damaged.

Eve Not damaged, no. I'm not a machine.

Celia You've got an incredible golden triangle right in the middle of your iris. Will I see you tomorrow?

Eve I'm meant to be doing a night shift.

Celia Tuesday, then?

Eve Tomorrow's fine. Perfect. Are you scared?

Celia I quite like to be scared. It's when I'm not that I start to worry.

Eve What do you mean?

Celia When the dust starts to settle.

Eve What do you mean about the dust settling?

Celia When things become familiar. Lazy.

Eve With your husband?

Celia With him as well.

Pause.

What?

Eve You haven't done this before. You said you hadn't.

Celia Because I haven't. With a woman. I've had affairs, darling. Just a few.

Eve Oh.

Pause.

Celia Oh, sweetheart. You look all hurt. It makes no difference to you, does it?

Eve What?

Celia We've neither of us been lily-white. What's happening is about us now not who's touched us or where in the past.

Celia strokes Eve's hair.

I haven't shocked you, have I? In the park. In the dark. You're sat with a posh floozy.

Pause.

You're surprised. And repelled.

Eve Surprised.

Celia And repelled.

Eve I'm not repelled.

Celia You're a bad liar. You'd never make a poker player.

Eve I don't want to be a poker player.

Celia Kiss me. (*Pause.*) Don't be so bloody conventional. I'm the same person now as I was three minutes ago.

Eve I know. I didn't say you weren't.

Celia Stop looking so beautifully judgemental then.

Eve kisses her; something has shifted a little.

Eve We'd better go. Don't want to get locked in.

Celia No. No. We absolutely don't want to get locked in.

They stand and walk out of the park.

SCENE FIVE

The Cains' parlour. Night. Celia sits, reading. William walks in, drunk.

William Books, is it?

Celia You're drunk?

William That's pretty obvious, isn't it? Why ask it like a question when in fact it's a comment. A judgement.

Celia Shall I ring for Hughes? He could make you some tea.

William I want no tea.

Celia Don't.

William Don't what? What am I not to do now?

Celia I'm going up. I'll see you in the morning.

William Inevitably. Are you aware that you stare into space more and more? It's like you've always desired a way to escape from it all. To defect. From the everyday routine. And you've finally found it. Some sort of transcendental something.

Celia I wasn't conscious of it. You must tell me when I do it again.

William Must I? There are many things you're not aware of. Go. Climb into that huge bed of yours.

Celia Have something to eat. Before you go to sleep.

William I don't want to eat.

Celia You'll feel better for it.

William That's rich. Coming from you. Bloody death camp. Where's my pipe? Where have they put it? If you refuse to eat in there. When you come out. There will be no home for you here.

Celia What?

William I may be tight but I'm in earnest.

William produces a written statement which he gives to Celia, who reads it.

Celia This is an ultimatum, is it? How long is my exile to last?

William You can stay with your mother. Live with your mother.

Celia You'd actually witness that? Me? And mother?

William I don't want you to leave our home. Neither do I want you to be butchered by a load of prison doctors. You seem to exhibit no sense of self-preservation whatsoever, consequence of which I am enforcing this condition. I concede that this might be a facile approach to what is loosely termed as protecting one's wife but that is in fact what I'm trying to do.

Celia And you'd cut me off. No home. No money.

William Yes. Exactly.

Celia If you had a sense of humour I'd think this were a joke.

William I have a brilliant sense of humour. It simply eludes you.

Celia William?

William Yes. (*Pause.*) What? Will you step down?

Celia No.

William There we are, then.

Celia I have borne you children. (*Pause.*) Seven children.

William Yes. I know you say I don't notice things, but that fact hadn't escaped my attention.

Celia And we have five children now.

William We do. What is your point?

Celia shakes her head.

I'm sorry.

Celia You're prepared to disown me, abandon me.

William Why do you always have to be so bloody melodramatic? This is Euston, not Sweden. I'm not forcing you into anything. What are you having?

William walks towards the drinks tray.

Celia I want a choice.

William Well, there's brandy or sherry or a pink gin.

William pours himself a drink.

I don't actually see why I should be ashamed or apologetic. I think it's all gone too far. That's simple enough, isn't it? I find the idea of women enduring torture obscene. And a young woman crumpled underfoot at the Derby repugnant. Unnecessary and sensationalist.

Celia You have no idea what it feels like. To be invisible.

William You all seem pretty bloody visible to me.

Celia You don't know.

William So tell me.

Celia You're asking me to tell you after more than twenty years together?

William Yes.

Celia You're drunk.

William Absolutely. I'm an inebriated brute. Without imagination. And of course utterly devoid of sensitivity. Go now. Close your bedroom door and pretend I'm a filthy figment of your imagination.

Celia William.

William And when you hear me crash into my room just pretend it's a beast, a friendly beast, exploring the life of bourgeois suburbia. It's quite normal. No need to be alarmed.

63

Celia Remember to put out the lights.

William You never cared for it, did you?

No reply.

I felt your cold sweat of relief every time it was done. I felt you reclaim yourself. Every time you pulled the sheets around you. And I heard you. Weeping. You put all your bodily effort into keeping your tears silent. So much so that I didn't dare turn around and ask you what was wrong. Or, perish the thought, try to touch you again. Sorry. I'm a beast. We're all beasts. Goodnight, Beauty. Go on. Piss off and leave me to my self-indulgence. 'Remember me at my best, Pip!'

Celia I will. I do.

William I do. I do I do I do I do. But you don't, do you?

Celia leaves. William goes to the drinks tray and pours himself another drink. He starts to walk towards a chair but stops and crouches down, settles on the floor. He gets up and goes to the gramophone, winds it up and puts the needle on the record. 'Oh You Beautiful Doll' plays, William sits and listens, he throws his glass at the wall.

SCENE SIX

Holloway Prison. The bath house. Evening. A line of women including Florence, virtually stripped, wait to enter several cowshed-type baths. A few of the women have small ragged towels with which they try to cover themselves. As women come out from behind the bath doors Briggs throws powder over them. They step on a scale where a Wardress records their weight and gives them a large clean handkerchief. There is a basket of random underclothes that the women then head for and huddle in a corner to get dressed in. Florence is almost naked, waiting to enter the bath. A Young Suffragette offers her towel to her. Mrs Briggs shouts.

Briggs Back! Back! Take it back!

Young Suffragette I don't need it. I . . .

Briggs Don't talk! Take it! Now!

Florence Who are you, Briggs?

Briggs No talking.

Florence No. Really. Who are you? How will you remember yourself when you're old? When you think of yourself as a young woman? Is this it?

Briggs I'll report you.

Florence I can't explain it to you, can I?

Briggs Quiet. Now.

Florence You should cherish your youth. When it's gone it's gone.

Florence gives the towel back to the Young Suffragette.

Thank you.

Briggs throws a towel towards Florence.

Briggs Pick it up then and no more talking.

Florence does not pick up the towel.

You're heading for isolation, you are. On your own.

The Young Suffragette picks up the towel and offers it to Florence, who does not take it, so the Young Suffragette gives it back to Briggs.

Florence You're a child, Sarah.

Briggs Briggs!

Florence I feel sorry for you.

Briggs I'm not a child. You're the one that's locked up in here. Not me.

Florence The walls are incidental. I'm a child too. I never said I wasn't. Just an older one. I'm going to have my bath now, then you can chuck that powder over me as if I were newborn.

Briggs Just don't talk, that's all.

Florence No. Absolutely. No.

Florence disappears into the bath shed. The other women look at Briggs.

SCENE SEVEN

A tea shop. Dusk. Celia and Eve sit together. Celia looks at the menu. Other couples are at various tables, including Mrs Major and her niece Felicity.

Celia I just think this once I should stand down. He's about to throw me out.

Eve I see that.

Celia Do you think I'm being awful?

Eve No.

Celia You could bunk off too.

Eve No. I got you something.

Eve puts a small gift on the table.

Celia You mustn't spend your money. Bugger. Could you move to the left a little. I've just seen Mrs Major. I can't bear the thought of saying hello. Don't look.

Eve glances over her shoulder then shuffles to her left.

Ta. Do you need some cash?

Eve What? No. Why?

Celia What? I don't see why you're prepared to do the most intimate things with me but as soon as I mention money you take umbrage.

Eve You'd probably take umbrage too, if it was the other way around.

Celia Do you know what the phrase means?

Eve What?

Celia Nothing. Let's open this.

The Waitress approaches.

Waitress Can I take your order, ladies?

Celia Could you give us a moment please? One slow minute?

Waitress Of course, miss. Is it your birthday?

Celia No – I don't have birthdays any more.

The Waitress smiles with Celia and leaves them.

Celia She called me 'miss'. How delicious. Charming uniforms, aren't they?

Eve looks away.

What? Oh, come on.

Celia unwraps the present. It is a cigarette case.

That's just beautiful. Thank you. Really. It's lovely. I've offended you.

Eve It wasn't the money. You just sounded . . . cold.

Celia I find a little coolness helps to put things in perspective.

Eve What? What do we need to put into perspective?

Celia Let's not ask the whole of the tea room, shall we?

Eve I thought you didn't care what other people thought.

Celia There's a time and a place.

Eve So where's ours? Our time. Our place. What's happening, Celia?

Celia Nothing. You've shifted.

Eve I haven't. Why do you say that?

Celia No. Your position darling. Left. Just a smidgen.

Eve stops, shifts her chair a little.

We're simply evolving.

Eve Can't we stay as we were?

Celia We can't remain as primitives, can we? Maybe it's your namesake. You hanker back to an age of innocence. It's quite a strange name to give a child, isn't it? When you think of what she did?

Eve My mother liked it.

Celia Ah yes, your mother. Well, that doesn't surprise me. Everyone's so beastly about poor Eve. I bet the garden would have become pretty dull if she hadn't rebelled. The two of them would have ended up bashing each other's skulls in with a spade if she hadn't transgressed. They'd have suffered irreparable brain damage. Then reeled around digging little burial pits for each other while they lost their minds.

The Waitress approaches.

Waitress Are you ready, miss?

Celia Yes. (*To Eve.*) Yes? We'd like two pots of tea and some sponge fingers, and do you have any *crème brûlée*?

Waitress Yes, miss.

Celia Splendid. All of that then. Times two. Like the ark.

The Waitress exits.

People lose their terror don't they? Once they've touched the area in between each other's legs. Love is just fear, I suppose. Masquerading as a fever. Then you explore each other and suddenly you have licence to become totally pedestrian. And ultimately abusive.

Eve Why are you saying this?

Celia (*indicating a couple at another table*) Look at those two. You'd think deciding what to eat or how much to tip the waiter was as important as the Rights of Man. It's a liquefied co-dependence. An amorphous mentality. Such a waste.

Eve We're not like that.

Celia Not yet.

Eve Why don't you just say if you don't want it?

Celia 'It' being what?

No reply.

If the 'it' is sexual relations with you then yes, I want it. If the 'it' is hiding and feeling perpetually frustrated then no, I don't want it.

Eve I'm in love with you.

Celia No. The reverence has gone. It's not something to mourn. It's rather liberating. Not to be worried about every pose you strike and every expression you make.

Eve It would be different if we were allowed to be together.

Celia Men and women are allowed to be together. And they're the worst of the lot.

No reply.

I risk everything here, Eve. We are in very different positions.

Eve I know. I know that.

Celia You'll be in Holloway within the week. For God knows how long.

Eve What do you want to say?

Celia I think it's better to part sooner than later.

Mrs Major approaches their table with a young niece, Felicity.

Mrs Major Lady Cain! I saw you! How are you? And the children? This is my niece Felicity. Deborah's gal.

Celia Oh, how marvellous. Hello, Felicity. This is Miss Douglas. Mrs Major, Felicity.

Mrs Major I heard about your son, how jolly, and they've chosen a perfect duck of a house, haven't they?

Celia They have.

Mrs Major (*to Eve*) You're wearing the badge! Good for you. Were you in for very long?

Eve shakes her head.

Good. Good. Well, we won't keep you. So pleasant, though. Do give my best to your family. Goodbye.

Celia Goodbye. Love to Dodo. Goodbye, Felicity.

Felicity Goodbye.

They exit. Celia looks at Eve. Pause.

Eve You said . . . part. Be apart.

Celia I don't want to waste your time. Or break your heart.

Eve Is that a line from one of your stories?

Celia Not yet, no.

Eve You sound like you rehearsed this.

Celia Important things should be rehearsed.

Celia pushes the cigarette case towards Eve.

Take this, darling. You use it. I'd prefer you to keep it.

Eve You think I'd use it? You've very little imagination for a writer. You should go. I feel like I'll say something awful.

Celia Say it. Please. You'll feel better if you say it.

Eve You'll feel better if I say it.

Celia Please.

Eve shakes her head.

I'm sorry if this has all been awkward. I'm rather a beginner, as you know.

Eve gets up and walks out. The Waitress comes over with cakes. Celia lights a cigarette, puts some money on the table and leaves.

SCENE EIGHT

A bedroom in the Ritz. Charlie stands by the window drinking wine. Celia sits, drinking. She lights a cigarette but does not smoke it. There is an empty wine bottle and a half-full one.

Charlie Looks beautiful from up here. The park. The lights. Don't it? How come you're staying here tonight?

Celia I've helped myself to your cigarettes. Do you mind?

Charlie Is this what you New Women do, is it?

Celia Stay in expensive hotels?

Charlie Invite the staff up? Is that your contribution towards democracy, is it?

Celia Do you like working here?

Charlie It has its moments. What sort of books do you write?

Celia Ghost stories.

Charlie No? Really? I've got an idea I always wanted to do. About a man in the fog. The streets he goes down. People he meets. Then he becomes the fog, he's in it and he becomes it.

Celia Are you drunk?

Charlie I'm intoxicated. By you.

Charlie inhales on his cigarette then lets the smoke out slowly.

Celia You're like a dragon.

Charlie I am a dragon. I've got great big teeth. And a giant tail. Why can't you go home, then? What did you do?

Celia I just can't.

Charlie Why did you invite me up here?

Celia Because you have a constant supply of cigarettes.

Charlie Can I sit next to you?

Celia I won't bite.

Charlie That's a shame. Sorry. I'm terrible. Have you done this before?

No reply. Charlie sits down next to Celia.

Can I just? To illustrate something?

He indicates his hand to her hip. Celia does not stop him.

Look at that.

He places his hand on her hip, then slowly follows the line to her thigh.

That curve there. And this one here. It's beautiful. Men are all straight lines. Angular. Like dead bodies already. Women. Look. You got this bit. And that. I can't imagine you laid out on a slab. Whereas I look halfway there. You gonna smoke that?

Charlie takes the cigarette from Celia and kisses her.

Celia No. Don't.

Charlie I thought this was what you wanted.

Celia No.

Charlie What then?

Celia I thought we might talk. About things.

Charlie Oh. What do you want to talk about?

Celia Anything.

Charlie Football?

Charlie stands up and moves away.

Celia I'm sorry. I'm confusing you.

Charlie You're very beautiful. I always thought that. When I saw you speak with your lot. In the park. Would you like me to leave?

Celia Thank you. For being a gentleman.

Charlie I'm not being a gentleman inside my head.

Celia I'm very lucky, aren't I? You might have been a brute.

Charlie How do you know I'm not?

Celia You liked the pictures on the stairwell.

Charlie Christ. You really know how to look after yourself, don't you?

Celia I had a bust up with my friend. She's . . . it's rather affected me.

Charlie You want some more Chablis?

Celia Please. She's rather cut up about it.

Charlie gets up, pours two glasses of wine and gives one to Celia.

Charlie Is she sick?

Celia Sick?

Charlie You're worried about her?

Celia Yes. I am. I'm all torn up.

Charlie Here's to you. Poor thing. Poor girl. You're in a bit of a state, aren't you?

He puts his arm around Celia.

Celia I don't really know what I'm doing.

Charlie Course you don't. That's alright.

He kisses her gently. Celia responds. Charlie caresses her.

Celia Yes.

Celia gives in to his embrace.

Charlie You're a right tart, aren't you?

Celia Yes. Possibly. Am I?

Charlie You don't know whether you're coming or going, do you? You won't even remember this tomorrow, will you?

Celia No. No, I hope not.

Charlie puts his hand up her skirts and negotiates the layers of underwear until he has passed them. Celia flinches.

Charlie Does that hurt?

Celia Yes.

Charlie Nice?

Celia No.

Charlie No?

Celia Really. Please. Don't.

Charlie I thought you'd like that.

Celia No.

Charlie Is that a real no or a pretend?

Celia Real.

Charlie takes his hand out from under her skirts.

Charlie I always wondered about women like you. What you'd be like underneath. You all smell the same.

Celia You should go now. Please. I think I'm going to puke.

Celia gets up and exits the room.

Charlie I'll wait for you. Make sure you're alright. Wait a bit. I'll make you better.

Charlie lights a cigarette.

SCENE NINE

Holloway Prison. An office. Morning. Celia and Eve sit on chairs. Celia is in smart civilian clothes, Eve is in her prison uniform.

Eve I don't want to feel this intensely ever again.

Celia Of course you do. And you will. You're young.

Eve I was never young.

Celia Why were you in isolation? Why?

No reply.

I brought you some cigarettes. I've been worried about you. Do you think we might get through this as friends?

Eve lights a cigarette.

Eve You've enough friends as it is.

Celia I don't, as it happens. Not real ones. I rather pretend to be more robust and popular than I really am. It snowed yesterday. Did you see it? I walked through the park and it was catching the sunshine as it fell. Strange how beauty moves one so easily, so visibly, yet one's so trapped when it comes to real emotions. I won't stay. It's not fair that I descend on you like this. A captive audience. I just wanted to see if I could bring you anything? . . . No. Goodbye.

Celia kisses Eve's cheek.

Eve I painted your name on the wall. With blood. I'd been striking for five days and it seemed like the thing to do.

Celia Blood? What blood?

Eve My blood. They stripped me. Looking for the cut. I feel bereft. Shabby.

Celia Well, you're not. Either of those things.

Celia picks up a prison-issue book then drops it to the floor.

Eve You could always write a story, 'Love among the Inverts'.

Celia Don't use that word. It's repulsive.

Eve 'Love'?

Celia I didn't ask you to fall in love with me. I actually warned you against it.

Eve True. Certain movements, signs, you made, could be interpreted as an invitation. If I could take one step away I could protect myself.

Celia I'll protect you.

Pause.

Eve You having a big Christmas?

Celia Florence and I are doing a bash at the Bow Canteen. Presents for all the children.

Eve You said our time together was interesting.

Celia Is that a crime, to find something interesting?

Eve Made it sound a bit like an experiment.

Celia I obviously can't say anything right. I should go.

Eve I'd like to write to you.

Celia You don't need to write to me.

Eve I know I don't need to. I'd like to.

Celia I'm not sure I'm in the right state of mind to receive a letter from you.

Eve Will you leave me your address?

Celia Just send it to the Union.

Eve You know my address. We were . . . together. Many times. In Limehouse. And you won't tell me where you live?

Celia Can I kiss you?

Eve looks away.

I imagined you might not live by the rules. But I think you do as much as the next person.

Eve Who is the next person?

Celia Desire is very strange. One shouldn't try to pin it down.

Eve I thought I heard you. Last week. I was at home. In bed. Late. I couldn't sleep. I was nervous. Foxes were barking. And I heard a woman singing in the square. And I thought you'd come back. That you were stood, down there on the pavement. Singing. I wanted to look out the window, but I didn't dare in case it wasn't you. Then the song stopped. And it was quiet. I thought you were waiting. That you'd shout something up to me. For me to run down to you. Then I jumped up and I looked out and there was no one there. Empty street. Yellow street lamp. Just some laughing round the corner and a bottle being smashed.

Celia I'm sorry I didn't come and sing to you.

Eve goes to the office door and shouts:

Eve Briggs? Can I go back to my cell now, please?

The door is opened and Eve walks out.

SCENE TEN

Holloway Prison. A doctor's office. Morning. An armchair.
A Wardress and a Nurse attend while a Guard escorts
Eve into the room. There are a few other Guards present.
Eve is led to a weighing machine which she stands on, then
gets off. A Guard records her weight. Dr Vale greets her.

Vale Morning. Do sit down.

Eve sits.

Where's the sheet?

Nurse Sorry, Doctor.

The Nurse lays down a white sheet under the chair
Eve sits down on. Vale listens to her heartbeat with
a stethoscope.

Vale How's your heart?

Eve Alright.

Vale Any other problems?

Eve No.

Vale refers to a blue piece of paper from his pocket.

Vale It says here that you are not to be released, even on
medical grounds. That you insist on refraining from food?

Eve Yes.

Vale Then I must compel you to take it.

Eve You've got to prove that I'm mad. You're not
allowed to perform any operation without a patient's
consent.

Vale bows.

Vale These are my instructions.

The Nurse approaches with a long red rubber tube attached to a funnel and a jug of liquid.

Nurse Excuse me, sir, Nurse Beaty is off today so I'm doing it instead. I've not been on before.

Vale The complications are invariably at my end, not yours. You've got about a pint there. You just watch that it's going down and let me know when it's finished, yes?

Nurse Yes sir. Thank you.

The Nurse stands on a chair to hold the apparatus, basically a funnel and a jug of liquid, while the Wardress and Guards stand at Eve's side. Vale prepares himself with a large apron and instruments.

Eve What's in it? What are you putting in me?

Vale Egg and brandy.

Eve I don't want it. I don't like it.

Vale This is not an hotel. If you don't want the stuff, you must simply resume eating. Right. Let's be having you. Don't start pouring until I give the say so, Nurse. And let me know when it's all gone, yes?

Nurse Yes, Doctor.

Wardress Do you want the gag, sir?

Vale No. Let her take it through the nose.

Vale pushes a tube into and up her nose. Eve bodily flinches and the Guards and Wardress hold her down. She is in severe pain, and trying to contain it, but her body is in spasms as Vale feeds it in and talks to the Nurse.

Come on. In you go. Come on. There. Have to push it in a good twenty inches, you see, Parker, so it goes right through to the stomach.

Nurse I see.

Vale You can start pouring now.

Nurse Yes sir.

The Nurse watches but does not pour the mixture.

Vale Yes?

She starts to pour, very slowly.

That's it. If ever you're on this end and it's not going down, you simply pinch the nose, yes? Is it going down?

Nurse Yes sir. Seems to be.

Vale Good. Good.

Eve's body shakes with the pain and she almost retches.

Gag. Get me the wooden gag.

The Wardress hands him the gag, which he forces into Eve's mouth. Eve spits it out and struggles.

Pass me the steel one. You, Parker, keep it there, tight, would you? Come on now. There's a good girl.

The Wardress passes Vale the steel gag, who gives it to Parker to hold steady in Eve's mouth. Eve heaves and chokes. They wait for one minute for all the liquid to go down. During this time Eve reaches different thresholds of pain.

Nurse It's gone, sir.

Vale Good. Well done. Now we just have to get the blasted thing out. Gently does it.

The Guard removes the gag. Vale gradually pulls the tube out slowly, which causes more pain than inserting it. Eve writhes and then stops, spent with pain. She lies motionless.

All done. Sit up now when you're ready. All yours, ladies.

Wardress Yes, sir.

The Wardress fetches a basin of water and starts to sponge Eve's chin and face. Vale bends in to look at Eve, who retches over him. He slaps her face.

Vale Stubborn. You must not be so stubborn.

Vale walks out, followed by Parker. The Wardress washes Eve's face then sprinkles her with some eau de cologne. The Nurse remains on the chair.

Wardress You can get down now.

The Nurse does not get down. The Wardress helps Eve to sit up. The Guard helps her gradually to stand.

Guard Do you want to stay put for a bit, girl? Before we go back? To pull yourself together?

Eve shakes her head, almost drugged by the pain. Eve takes his arm and the Wardress takes her other arm. Eve looks beaten, worn, but also like a child, vulnerable. She nods her head and they start to walk together out of the office.

SCENE ELEVEN

Celia's parlour. Dusk. Celia is looking in drawers. William walks in.

William Where have you been?

Celia I stayed with a friend.

William We've all been worried bloody sick. Telephoning the police station. Hospitals.

Celia Sorry. I can't find my spectacles.

William Is that it? 'Sorry'?

Celia You don't think Liza would have put them in my room, do you? Please don't go into the sulks. I've rather had enough of all that.

William I thought you might be dead.

Celia I probably was.

William Could you just for once not speak in code?

Celia I wanted to have one night of my life unaccounted for. Is that clear enough? Is that permissible? Just a few hours where nobody knew where I was. I thought it might be a little like Heaven. Being anonymous for a moment. Actually it wasn't very pleasant. And I was the loneliest I've ever felt. Do you feel any better now? Knowing that my selfish oblivion was actually repugnant? You're about to throw me onto the streets. I would have thought my behaviour was pretty typical under the circumstances.

William Who were you with last night?

Celia I already told you. Do you want names? Addresses?

William Christ, you're selfish.

Celia I think we've covered this ground before, haven't we?

William It's not clever. To hurt people. I don't know why you're scouring my desk. They won't be in there.

Celia picks up a photograph.

Celia I didn't realise you were so sentimental. What's this one called? 'Wife, Pre-Conversion'?

William Don't maul my stuff, thanks.

Celia picks up another photograph.

Celia God. Us on the boat. On your tenth birthday. Coming back from Calais. In that storm. I was terribly sick, wasn't I? Retching over the side.

William Where did you stay?

Celia You held my hair away from my face.

William Where were you?

Celia At the Ritz.

William I just don't understand why you want to make me worry.

Celia Nor do I, Will. Nor do I. I'm sorry. That you worried. I'm sorry.

William Are you drunk?

Celia It depends how long the effects last. You should be able to answer that one. I've not had a drink this morning, if that's what you're asking.

William Why the bloody Ritz, for Christ's sake?

Celia I fancied a view of the park. I thought you'd know it was just me swanning off. One of my gestures.

William I'm not Houdini.

Celia I think he escapes rather than reads minds.

William How was breakfast there? Is it all it's cracked up to be?

Celia It was very good. I watched the soldiers riding, saw the red of their uniforms flash through the trees. From my window. Very early. Beautiful huge black horses. And they were just running everywhere. It was so wonderful to see them not in formation. I'd forgotten they could be like that. Dust flying up and their swords kept catching the first of the winter sunshine. I felt I might run out there and become part of a tragedy.

William I'm sorry it hasn't been all you hoped for.

Celia I can't change.

William No, of course you can't. It's a ridiculous notion. But I can't climb the walls, you see? So I'm redundant. Those bloody great big grey stones. I'm not attacking you. You simply have no notion, do you? Of how that feels.

Celia You seem different.

William Do I? No. I'm the same.

Celia I have tried. To make a good marriage. I just don't really know how.

William I worry. I do worry. About you.

William breaks down. Celia holds him.

SCENE TWELVE

Eve's lodgings. Late afternoon. There is a white enamel basin of water on the floor. Eve is in her Sunday dress. She takes it off. Then sponges herself clean. She puts the Sunday dress on the floor with the basin in front of her. She picks up the dress and holds it as if it were a person, then puts it down. She crouches by the basin, picks up a cut-throat razor that is next to it. She puts her hands into the basin, cuts her wrists, blood fills the water.

SCENE THIRTEEN

Holloway Prison. The hospital. Afternoon. Women lie in hospital beds. Eve is in bed, her wrists bandaged. Florence enters with a basket of provisions and the Suffragette *magazine. She approaches the Nurse near to Eve.*

Florence Briggs said I could come in for a short while. For Miss Douglas.

Nurse Bed number three. Five minutes.

Florence sits by Eve's bedside.

Florence It's me. Florence Boorman. Don't move. Just . . . What can I get for you? Water? Anything?

Eve Nothing, Miss Boorman.

Florence Florence. So . . . we'll just sit, then. Time will help. It does. Believe me. The hospital ward's as bureaucratic as ever, eh? And one young nurse didn't know what the Union was. I shall tell her before I leave. Celia's not here?

Eve Gone. To get some tea.

Florence Good. Tea is always good.

Eve How's your motor car?

Florence Splendid. Yes, it's splendid. Thank you.

Eve Sorry. I'm very sorry.

Florence takes Eve's hand. They are silent together. Celia enters with two cups of tea.

Celia Flo. Thanks for coming. I'd have got you a cup. Have mine.

Florence No no. Well, Miss Douglas is looking just fine, isn't she?

Celia I've seen you look better. I'm only allowed another few minutes, Flo.

Florence I only came to collect you and to say hello to the wounded soldier. I've brought some things. There's *The Suffragette*.

She takes the Suffragette *magazine out of her basket.*

Perhaps I'll give that to the nurse, shall I? I'll wait by the gate. Goodbye, Eve.

Celia Thanks, Flo.

Eve Night.

Florence leaves.

Celia It's not night, sweetheart. It's day. Can you see that?

Eve Mm.

Celia Can you see my hand? It's not dark.

Celia puts her hand near to Eve's face. Eve takes Celia's hand and puts it against her cheek. Celia sits next to Eve and puts her other hand on Eve's brow.

Eve You.

Celia You've cooled down a little. You were burning up. While you were asleep. Flo's left you some cakes. Christ. Cakes . . . We'll get you out of here as soon as we can.

Celia takes Eve's hand. Eve looks at her own hand.

You silly girl. Eve. You stupid, stupid . . . Sorry.

Eve I've got tiny holes, look. From the machine.

Celia No, there's no holes. You've had a fever. Could you drink some water, do you think?

Eve I used to run back from work along the marshes. Birds. Frogs. To meet you. I'd lie on my floor. In the sun.

Celia Eve. Promise me one thing.

Eve I thought you were singing that night. In the square.

Celia I should have been singing. I'm sorry.

Eve Are you going?

Celia I have to.

Eve I was very proud. To be with you.

Celia And I was proud to be with you. Terribly proud.

Nurse Time, Lady Cain.

Celia Please, we're just . . .

Eve I'm not ready to go.

Celia You're not going anywhere, darling.

Eve I haven't got my coat. Are my hands bleeding?

Celia No. No, they're not. They're not. They're not. They're not.

Celia kisses Eve's hands. Celia weeps. Eve strokes Celia's head.

Eve It's alright. It's alright.

Nurse Time, miss.

Celia kisses Eve on the forehead and leaves. The Nurse feels Eve's pulse and records it.

SCENE FOURTEEN

Florence's parlour. Evening. Celia sits with a drink at her side, cutting material for a banner. Florence enters with her coat and hat on. She takes her hat and gloves off.

Florence You're still here.

Celia He's late.

Florence Two hours late.

Celia Sorry, Flo. Am I in the way?

Florence No.

Celia Maybe he's changed his mind.

Florence After months of calling here like a schoolboy? He's been as nervous as a kitten. How's that going?

Celia Slow. I couldn't find your good scissors. Any news?

Florence finds her good scissors and gives them to Celia.

Florence No. But Hardie says he'd rather shoot his sons than let them become soldiers if war's declared.

Celia Schliefke called for you. Said I was to pass on the message that we're to shut down and become patriots if it happens.

Florence I saw Eve Douglas. On the Strand.

Celia Did you?

Florence We had tea.

Celia Ah. Good. How did she seem?

Florence Quite well. She's to be married. To a watch maker.

Celia Oh.

Florence Yes. In June.

Celia Bertie's adamant that he'll become a hero. Madeline's urging him to go off and return to her *couvert de gloire*. Bloody idiot. Did she seem well?

Florence She was alright. Her health's not great.

Celia pours herself another drink. There is a knock at an outside door. And a bell.

Celia William.

Florence I'll get it.

Celia What's wrong with her?

Florence She didn't go into specifics.

Florence goes to answer the door.

Celia Did she look happy?

Florence No.

Celia Was he with her?

Florence No. He was working. In Walthamstow. I've some leafleting to do. Wednesday?

Celia Yes. Thanks, Flo.

Florence takes her hat and leaves. Celia lights a cigarette. She puts a record on the phonograph. Mozart. William enters.

William Celia.

Celia nods, tries to smile.

I'm sorry I'm late. Is that everything in the hall?

Celia Yes. There's heaps of stuff, I'm afraid. Most of it's rubbish. I don't know how or why I've amassed it in three months.

William Are you alright?

Celia nods. She takes the needle off the record. William goes to her and tries to hold her, gently kiss her; it's all a bit awkward.

Celia How was your day?

William It was good. Very good. You look nice.

Celia You go on, Will. I'll be there in a moment.

William picks up her coat for her. He holds it for her to put on but she takes it from him.

William Coat.

Celia Yes. Yes, it is.

William leaves. Celia puts on her coat. She buttons it up and reaches for her hat. She is about to put it on, checking herself in the mirror, when she breaks down. She puts the record on to muffle her crying and holds herself. She now controls herself. She wipes her face and checks herself in the mirror. William walks in.

William Are you ready?

Celia Yes.

William looks at her, sees she has been crying and kisses her cheek. He passes her his handkerchief. Celia sits down. She drinks her wine. William sits next to her. He takes her hand.

William Your hand's like ice.

William covers her hand with both of his. Then breathes on it to make it warmer.

Celia Do you remember when we stayed at Yuri's dacha? We ran away from the other children playing in the evening. Into the woods. And we saw the wolf? And we watched it. And he started to walk towards us? And we both stood absolutely still. The only thing moving was our breath. And then very slowly you took my hand. Do you remember? Do you?

They sit for a few moments in silence.

William You're not coming home.

Pause. William stands and walks away from Celia. He pours himself a brandy.

Celia I thought I was. I really did.

William What made you change your mind? When did you decide this?

Celia I don't know.

William Where will you go?

Celia That wolf. It was so beautiful, Will. It broke my heart it was so beautiful.

William downs his drink and leaves. The outside door slams. Celia lights another cigarette. She smokes, reaches for her hat, puts it on. She checks herself in the mirror and leaves.

Large images of various Suffragettes come onto a screen, some together, some alone: prison images, their hair down, defiant, timeless.

Blackout.